COVER LETTERS

Made Easy

Patty Marler ■ Jan Bailey Mattia

Printed on recyclable paper

AULT PUBLIC LIBRARY
AULT, COLORADO

VGM Career Horizons
a division of *NTC Publishing Group*
Lincolnwood, Illinois USA

It is easy to begin the pursuit of a dream; to accomplish
it takes the endless help and support of family and friends.
For this we thank each of you.

Library of Congress Cataloging-in-Publication Data

Marler, Patty.
    Cover letters made easy / Patty Marler, Jan Bailey Mattia.
        p.   cm.
    ISBN 0–8442–4346–9 (pbk.)
    1. Cover letters.   2. Applications for positions.   I. Mattia, Jan
Bailey. II. Title.
HF5383.M288   1996
808'.06665—dc20   95–30110
                                       CIP

Published by VGM Career Horizons, a division of NTC Publishing Group
4255 West Touhy Avenue
Lincolnwood (Chicago), Illinois 60646–1975, U.S.A.
© 1996 by NTC Publishing Group. All rights reserved.
No part of this book may be reproduced, stored in a retrieval
system, or transmitted in any form or by any means,
electronic, mechanical, photocopying, recording or otherwise,
without the prior permission of NTC Publishing Group.
Manufactured in the United States of America.

5 6 7 8 9 0 VP 9 8 7 6 5 4 3 2 1

Contents

Introduction

Your cover letter is the first thing an employer sees and thus is a vital part of your resume package. It must catch an employer's attention, describe why you are perfect for a position, and encourage the recipient to continue on to your resume. Given the importance of the cover letter, it is easy to see why writing one can make a person nervous.

"Do what you can, with what you have, where you are."

—Theodore Roosevelt

Cover Letters Made Easy will take you through the process of creating an exceptional cover letter. We begin by looking at the **top 20 openers . . . to get your cover letter read,** lines which are sure to capture employers' attention and keep them reading. We then discuss why it is so important to have a good letter in the chapter titled **why a cover letter?**

Cover letter varieties looks at the many different ways of creating and using letters, and discusses which are most effective. The section on **what employers look for** will get you started on making a great first impression. Then the process of creating a letter which is sure to get you noticed is outlined in **cover letter know-how.**

The difference between what you say and what employers may read is looked at in **employer translations,** and **putting it all together** describes various options for the final product. From there we give you examples of **the good, the bad, and the ugly** in the world of cover letters.

Finally, we finish by providing **sample cover letters** that will further inspire you to write your own great cover letter!

Special Features

Special features that appear throughout the book will help you pick out key points and apply your new knowledge.

 Notes clarify text with concise explanations.

 Helpful Hints make you stand out in the crowd of job seekers.

 Vocab Rehab suggests ways to spice up your cover letter so that it not only describes your talents effectively, but is interesting to read as well.

 Special Thoughts provide inspiration and motivation.

It's time to get started—your new job awaits you!

Top 20 Openers . . . To Get Your Cover Letter Read

Your cover letter needs a strong opening sentence to grab employers' attention and encourage them to continue reading. Replace openings which bore employers stiff, like "I am submitting my resume in response to your ad in the daily newspaper" or "I am sending you a copy of my resume," with interesting and engaging openers.

1. Six years experience and a Bachelor of Arts degree with a major in Political Science make me well qualified to fill your journalist position.

2. I am a reliable, productive, adaptable, and enthusiastic person who follows through on ideas and suggestions.

"It may be those who do most, dream most."

—Stephen Leacock

3. Committed, hard-working, and thorough are words my past employers use to describe me. I would bring all these to Scheffield Brothers if hired.

4. It is with considerable interest and enthusiasm that I am applying for the position of travel consultant with the Travel Network.

Loudly blow your own horn and be completely and totally boastful when you write your opening sentence. Then go back and see if it needs to be toned down. You will probably be surprised to find it sounds confident and self-assured, not arrogant or obnoxious.

5. I am a highly motivated person with tireless enthusiasm and energy, and am warmly regarded by fellow workers.

6. I have built a solid reputation for initiative, accuracy, and attention to detail—all essential skills for a junior accounting clerk.

"Confidence is a plant of slow growth."

—William Pitt

7. "Creative and accepting of whatever challenge is given" is how my previous employer describes my character.

8. Thank you for your encouragement and for answering my questions when we spoke on the telephone yesterday. Please find my resume detailing my skills related to the workshop facilitator position.

9. I am an excellent salesperson and possess the skills to help your company grow and build repeat clientele.

10. I am pleased to respond to your advertisement regarding the office manager position. I welcome the opportunity to use my interpersonal and administrative support skills in an interesting and challenging environment.

"Don't stand shivering upon the bank; plunge in at once and have it over."

—**T.C. Haliburton**

11. Further to our telephone conversation on October 5, I am enclosing my resume which outlines my skills in the woodworking field in greater detail.

12. I offer a successful background in customer service with extensive sales, marketing, and promotions experience.

13. I am a well-organized and productive individual who displays excellent initiative and follow-through.

14. I have an excellent foundation in legal proceedings, word processing, and research skills, and believe I possess the qualifications required to fill the legal secretary position to your complete satisfaction.

Use a thesaurus to find descriptive words to characterize yourself, such as "energetic," "excel at," "conscientious," and "eager."

15. Along with my experience and training, I have many personal attributes which make me an excellent candidate for the social worker position.

16. I am an individual with outstanding public relations abilities. My experience, qualifications, and professional manner would be advantageous to your company.

17. Eight years of administrative experience and strong organizational and interpersonal skills prompt me to submit my resume for consideration in the competition for human resources assistant.

18. I was pleased to learn of an opportunity within your organization for a well-organized individual with excellent data entry skills, customer service abilities, and the proven commitment to work independently.

"Success is seldom achieved by those who contemplate possibilities of failure."

—Smith Adams

19. I am a dedicated and responsible person who serves the customer and my company well.

20. Detailed in my resume you will find a solid clerical background that includes data entry, word processing, and customer service skills. These skills combine to make me an excellent choice for your executive assistant position.

Chapter 1

Why A Cover Letter?

A good cover letter is short, to the point, and has impact. This can make it a difficult part of your "resume package" to write. It is equally if not more important than your resume, as it is the first impression an employer receives of you, the impression that helps them decide if they should continue reading.

Try starting sentences with, "As a dedicated employee I . . ." rather than "I am a dedicated employee . . .". Not only do you avoid the repetitive "I am" statement, it encourages you to describe in what ways you are a dedicated employee.

In the past, the cover letter was used only as a formality and to ensure your resume landed in the correct pile for the correct position. It still has the same purpose today, but its role has also expanded considerably.

The cover letter, in a few short paragraphs, can accomplish many things.

What?

Introduction

This is perhaps the most general reason for a cover letter. It is a brief overview of you, your skills, and why you are interested in the company.

All cover letters introduce you, but you may develop an introductory letter whose sole purpose is to create interest in you and not try at this point to do anything beyond that.

"If there is no wind . . . Row."

—Latin proverb

Directing focus

An excellent cover letter can direct an employer's attention wherever you need, or want, it to go. A great letter not only highlights important information but draws attention away from information that might lessen your chances for an interview.

Have someone else read your cover letter to you out loud. Do you still like the way it sounds? Do they?

Re-establish the link

If you have done your networking well, you will have spoken to the employer prior to sending in a resume. Your cover letter can serve to remind them of your conversation, what you discussed, and why they should be interested in you.

For ideas on how to network effectively see *Job Hunting Made Easy.*

Highlight skills

Although your resume should explain your skills in detail, a good cover letter works to highlight those areas of your experience you feel are most suited to the job you are applying for. These are the skills that will land your resume in the interview pile.

Employers are intrigued by strong words in you cover letter. "Hard-working," "dedicated," "team player," "initiative," "results-oriented" are words more likely to grab an employers attention than "I think I would do a good job."

Create curiosity

An employer faced with hundreds of resumes will be most likely to put yours in the "keeper" pile if your cover letter is interesting to read and to look at. A dynamic and well-written cover letter will make an employer want to look at your resume to learn a little more about you.

"Behold the turtle. He makes progress only when he sticks his neck out."

—James Bryant Conant

Fill the gaps

If you are not able to customize your resume for a job application, you can use your cover letter to fill in the gaps. Perhaps you are enrolled in a course directly related to the job and it is not on your resume. Mention it in your letter. You may have a chronological resume listing only job duties. This type of resume may not say much about you as an individual and you will want to include more personal information in your cover letter.

Whenever possible, customize your resume for the position you are applying for.

The possibilities are endless for illustrating your skills and experience in a cover letter. The challenge is to keep it short and interesting at the same time.

It really is quite amazing what a well-written cover letter can accomplish. It is equally amazing what a poorly written cover letter can undo!

You may find it frustrating when you first start writing cover letters. It seems as though there is so much to say and only a few short lines to say it in. *Keep at it.* For an employer, an excellent cover letter is a blessing to receive and to read. For you, an excellent cover letter may mean having the resume you worked so hard on read . . . or not.

Keep a file of all the cover letters you write. You can learn from them and you may be able to use sentences or ideas over again.

Chapter 2

Cover Letter Varieties

A cover letter is a cover letter is a cover letter, and one is as good as the next, right? Not so. There are many ways you can put your letter together, and they are not all equally effective.

"How busy is not so important as why busy. The bee is praised; the mosquito is swatted."

—Author unknown

Form Letters

Now that you realize how important it is to have a good cover letter, it might seem that the best thing to do is create *one* good cover letter that says it all. This way you can use it over and over again, no matter what the position. This is the best way to approach cover letters, right?

Wrong!

The reason you have a cover letter is to spark an employer's interest and describe why you are perfect for a particular job. Standard form letters are too general and don't effectively highlight your expertise for a specific position.

Think about form letters you receive in the mail, addressed to "Dear Sir or Madam." Chances are you throw them in the garbage before you finish reading them. Do you want employers to do this with your cover letter?

You may be tempted to create a standard cover letter because:

→ You only have to write one letter, and if writing isn't your strongest skill, it's easier to do one letter which sounds good and send it to every employer.

→ All the jobs you apply for are similar, so there is bound to be something in the cover letter that will be useful to an employer.

→ You always have a cover letter on hand so you can photocopy and submit one at any time.

Photocopies can looked washed out and be hard to read. Cover letters that look bad are likely to be skipped.

→ You don't have your own computer and going to the library when you want to create a customized letter is a hassle.

→ Your skills are in your resume, so why should you put them in a cover letter?

Employers may receive as many as 200 cover letters and resumes for any given position. Cover letters which are hard to read or which are boring form letters may be immediately excluded from the competition without the resume ever being read.

→ Frank down the road used a form letter and he got a job!

Although you may be tempted to create a standard letter to photocopy and submit with every resume, this is the least effective way of introducing your skills to employers. Don't limit your chances by submitting a form letter which is too general or describes irrelevant skills.

 An employer wants to know the talents, experience, and personal characteristics which make you good for the position with their company. Don't leave the employer with the impression you aren't interested enough in a job to take the time to write a letter specifically for them.

Modified Cover Letters

The only difference between modified and standard cover letters is that modified ones leave blank spaces to fill in the employer's name and available position.

Dear _____,

I am applying for the _____ position with your company.

These letters let the company know what you are applying for, but have the same drawbacks as the standard cover letters. They may even be worse because along with being too general, they look bad.

"Before the gates of excellence the high gods have placed sweat."

—Greek Proverb

Modified cover letters look unprofessional because:

➜ The printer ribbon on your typewriter may print darker or lighter than the original, so it is easy to see you have filled in the blanks.

➜ The name and position may not line up with the rest of the text, drawing attention to the fact that you simply filled in the blanks.

➜ The information you add may not fit in the space you allowed, or there may be too much room left over.

There is no way to fill in the appropriate information and still have the letter look clean and professional. No matter what you do, it is always obvious you have just filled in the blanks. Don't use this kind of letter.

 If you are taking the time to fill in the blanks, take the time to type a completely new letter. It will look better and be more likely to impress an employer.

ustomized Cover Letters

Descriptive, relevant, and personal—customized letters are your best choice! When you develop a new letter for each position, you give yourself the opportunity to sell yourself most effectively to employers.

 If you submit the same resume for each position you apply for, it is especially important to develop customized cover letters. They outline your specific qualifications related to the position. The employer doesn't have to sift through your resume to find out what makes you good for the job.

Customized letters:

➡ Draw attention to your most relevant skills and experience.

➡ Don't waste the employer's time by describing skills which aren't relevant to the position.

➡ Pique an employer's interest and encourage him or her to continue on to your resume.

➡ Are addressed to the person in charge of hiring and show that you have taken the time to discover his or her name.

➡ Look good.

You may have similar information or even the same opening or closing sentence in your customized cover letters, but the core information must be specific to the position you are applying for.

Because customized letters take more time and effort to write, people often avoid them.

Remember: The letter written for a specific position is most effective and is more likely to get you an interview.

Identify the skills you want to highlight ahead of time so you have a starting point when customizing your letters.

Example:
Mcgrath Printing is looking for a typesetter to set manuscripts which contain text and graphics.

Christine sees the ad and writes a cover letter addressed to Terri Brown, the employer at Mcgrath Printing, and refers to the typesetting position in her letter. She describes her typing accuracy and speed and states she has taken typesetting courses. She outlines her experience working on various computer design programs, her knowledge of the printing industry, and her desire to work in the field.

Pat, who is equally qualified for the position, submits the cover letter she wrote when she began looking for work. It outlines her typing speed and clerical experience, and states she is willing to accept any position. Because it is a photocopied letter there is no reference made to her knowledge of the work Mcgrath does or to the volunteer work Pat herself has done recently on the community newspaper.

As an employer for Mcgrath Printing, which person would you consider interviewing??

"The greatest pleasure in life is doing what people say you cannot do."

—Walter Bagehot

Now that you see how valuable it is to customize your cover letters, take the time to write a new cover letter for each position you apply for. The results will be worth your effort.

Chapter 3

What Employers Look For

Making your cover letter perfect, dynamic, easy to read, catchy, professional looking, short and to the point is hard work. Will an employer even read it?

Yes!

Although an employer may not sit and contemplate every word you have written in your letter, they do look for specific things.

Qualifications

Highlight the qualifications you have which match what the employer is looking for.

This will probably be the first thing an employer will skim through and look for in your letter. Be sure it is there.

Do not draw attention to skills you do not have, for example, by saying, "although I have no formal training . . ." Instead, highlight the experience you do have. An employer looks at you as a package. What you lack in education you may make up for in experience. Do not under-sell yourself!

Personality

Reflect who you are without sounding pompous or egotistical.

A good letter gives an employer an impression of you as a person as well as a potential employee.

 **Be careful if you intend to use humor in your cover letter. Remember, an employer cannot see your face when they read your letter and may not get what was intended as a joke. Trying to use humor or sound too familiar or casual with an employer can backfire making you sound frivolous or silly, so beware!**

Length

Keep your letter brief and to the point.

If your letter is longer than one page, you can be sure an employer will read only the first half and maybe the last sentence or two. If you find yourself writing that much in your cover letter, you should take a look at revising your resume to include the extra information.

 One page is an *absolute* maximum for a cover letter.

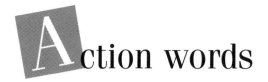ction words

You need to come across as someone who would be a dynamic asset to the company, someone the employer would want as a member of their team. Use action words to do this.

Action words are energetic words which make you sound like a go-getter, someone who would work hard for the company and would accept any challenge offered.

 See the section of dynamic descriptions in Chapter 4 for action word examples.

resentation

Make your letter interesting to look at and to read.

 Italicize or put in bold type the key words you use which were in the ad. This makes them stand out and captures the employer's attention.

Your cover letter must be organized, easy to read, professional looking, and free of errors. It must also suit the type of employment you are seeking.

Examples:

If you are applying to be an interior designer, an employer will look for your creative expression in a cover letter. Don't be afraid to submit a cover letter which is different, one that is unique yet still professional.

If you are applying to be an executive secretary, employers will scour your letter for spelling, typing, and grammatical errors. Be sure they won't find any!

 Instead of closing your cover letter with "Sincerely" or "Yours Truly," try using an interesting yet professional closing remark, such as "Eager to become a member of your team," "I look forward to hearing from you," or "Enthusiastically."

Handwritten Cover Letters

Cover letters should always be composed on a computer or typewriter; they are easier to read, more professional, and generally look better.

 Children in school receive lower grades if their reports are not completed on a computer or typewriter. You too will be "graded" lower for submitting a handwritten cover letter.

The only time you should consider submitting a handwritten letter is when an employer specifically asks for one. Interestingly enough, some employers do ask.

Why?

There are a few reasons why employers might ask for handwritten cover letters.

1. A great deal can be learned about a person by the way they write. Is your handwriting flamboyant and creative? Or is it small and efficient with no extra expression? Does it all slant in one direction or does it flip back and forth?

   Every handwriting style says something about the person who creates it. Some employers feel they can find out more about a person by observing their penmanship. Take a look at your handwriting and see what it says about you. You may be surprised to discover how well it matches your personality!

Paperclip a piece of lined paper behind the unlined piece you want your handwritten cover letter on. Your finished letter will look better on unlined paper, and this will give you a guide when you are writing.

2. Most people have a tendency to edit and rewrite less when they handwrite something as opposed to composing it on a computer. An employer may feel that by seeing a handwritten letter they see the "real" you.

"I was taught that the way of progress is neither swift nor easy."
—Marie Curie

3. Computers have spelling and grammar checkers. It takes a little more work to create an error-free handwritten letter and employers want to see if you are capable of doing it well.

   Regardless of the reason they want a handwritten cover letter, if employers requests one, then that is what you should give them. Be certain to consider all the same things you would if you were using a computer. Write and rewrite it as many times as you need to make sure it is perfect.

If you do make an error writing your letter, do not simply cross it out and keep going. Start over on a fresh piece of paper.

Summing Things Up

All of these elements are important considerations when you are writing your cover letter. Be prepared to write your letters several times until you have one that sounds like you, looks good, and describes you in precisely the way you want it to. Employers do look at cover letters. A great cover letter is truly a blessing for an employer as well as an asset for you!

Chapter 4

Cover Letter Know-How

Yes, the cover letter is a short, one page letter. Nevertheless, it's a letter all in its own category and it takes a lot of practice to write a great one.

 Learn to use connector words so you don't have a letter that says "I am" and "I have" over and over again. For examples: "In addition, my experience includes . . . ," "With my proven," "As a result, my . . . ."

Why?

In just a few short paragraphs you must describe yourself and your skills in enough detail to show an employer they would be missing out if they didn't call you in for an interview.

Your letter must be:

- interesting
- informative
- easy to read
- pleasing to look at
- without error
- efficiently to the point

There is a lot of pressure riding on this short, one-page summary of your experience. Be prepared to rewrite it a number of times before it is perfect.

"If you don't learn from your mistakes there's no sense making them."

—Laurence J. Peter

The Fine Details

Begin the process of writing your customized letter by gathering as much information as possible about the company. The fine details you gather are important to having a complete and accurate letter, one which is sure to impress an employer.

What?

1. The company's complete name.

    Addressing your letter to *Shorty's* is not good enough when the full company name is *Shorty's Specialty Clothing*. Show that you know something about the company. Start by using their name correctly.

"Better ask twice than go wrong once."

—German proverb

2. The company's correct address.

    You want your cover letter and resume for an "operator" to go to the local telephone company, not the local hospital. Locate and note the correct address.

3. The person responsible for hiring.

    Each cover letter should be addressed to a specific individual. If a company name is given in the advertisement, call and ask to whom you should address your letter. This also gives you a contact name when you call to ask about the position.

 Find out how the person prefers to be addressed and ask for the correct spelling of his or her name. It is surprising the impact this has on an employer—and even more surprising how few people do it!

Examples:

From: Dear Human Resource Manager,

Dear Hiring Supervisor,

Dear Sir/Madam,

To Whom It May Concern,

To: Dear Kathy Johnson,

Dear Ms. Johnson,

Dear Ms. Kathy Johnson,

4. The job title and reference number.

    Quote the job title *exactly* and include the reference number so the human resources department knows where to direct your application package. Many resumes are discarded because no one knows which position they are for.

    If you are not applying for a particular job opening, identify the type of work you are interested in. This way your resume can be directed to a specific supervisor or kept on file for future reference.

Rather than saying "I would be interested in any kind of work," say "I am interested in a position in the widget-making field." The employer will see that you have a career goal.

Gathering these details for your cover letter is easy if you have an advertisement, job description, or information about a position. If you do not, pick up the telephone, call the company, and start asking questions.

Remember, the better the letter, the better your chances for getting an interview.

WORKSPACE: THE FINER DETAILS

Company's name

_____

_____

_____

_____

Company's address

_____

_____

_____

_____

Person responsible for hiring

_____

_____

_____

_____

Job title and reference number

_____

_____

_____

_____

Before the Beginning . . .

The idea of writing a cover letter can seem overwhelming when you think of all the information and experience you would like to include. You'll find the process less painful if you simply start, rather than spend time contemplating how difficult it is going to be. Once you get some ideas down on paper, it will be easier to edit, expand, and rearrange.

"You can't turn back the clock but
you can wind it up again."

—Bonnie Prudden

How?

Read The Advertisement

An employer usually outlines the specific qualifications they are looking for in the ad. The more of these you can match with your experience, the better. These will probably be the specific skills the employer will look for when skimming your cover letter.

If you do not have a particular qualification an employer is looking for, do not mention or dwell on it. Your time is better served highlighting the experience you do have, not trying to explain the experience you do not have.

Review Your Resume

This is a good way to refresh your memory and determine the focus of your cover letter. You will be reminded of elements in your resume you want to draw the employers attention to, as well as skills or experience that are not in your resume that you should highlight.

It is best to customize each resume you drop off. If you can't, your cover letter can be used to fill in gaps in your resume.

Review Old Cover Letters

If you have cover letters from past positions for which you have applied, take a look at them. You may find a well-written cover letter with information in it that applies to the current position you are seeking. Or you may find an old cover letter that is poorly written. Reviewing it will give you a good idea of what you don't want to say! Either way, you will have learned something.

Keep a copy of each cover letter you submit. Write follow-up dates and details of things you want to remember for when an employer calls you back.

Review Letters of Reference

An excellent way to get in the mood to write about how great you are in a cover letter is to read how great someone else thinks you are in a reference letter! You may find a sentence or two you can borrow which describes your appropriate skills, or you may simply be reminded of qualities and experiences you should mention.

If you use a statement from a letter of reference, highlight it so an employer knows where it comes from. For example, "I am a "highly motivated person with tireless enthusiasm and energy and am warmly regarded by staff." This is how my previous employer describes me." This will impress a potential employer.

Now you have everything you need. You know what the employer is looking for, you know what relevant experience you have, and you know how great previous employers thought you were. There is no better time to start!

"He has half the deed done who has made a beginning."

—Horace

In the Beginning . . .

Although you must try to be creative as well as professional when writing your cover letter, there are three basic components to include in your letter: the opening sentence, the body, and the closing. The length of each component will vary with every letter, but for your letter to read well, they should all be included to some degree.

While writing your letter, read and re-read the advertisement or job description, if you have one. Sometimes when writing about ourselves we tend to get side-tracked. This will help keep you focused.

Opening Sentence:

You must have a dynamic opening sentence to spark an employer's interest. Do not begin with, "I am submitting my resume in response to your ad in The Paper for the position of . . . "

Why?

The employers are aware that you are submitting a resume, they know where and when they advertised, and most of all, such an opening says nothing about you and why you should be hired for the position. Think of your opening statement as your first impression in an interview. It must have impact!

"The marvelous richness of human experience would lose something of rewarding joy if there were no limitations to overcome."

—Helen Keller

A dynamic, attention-grabbing opening sentence describes your strongest skills and attributes, how they relate to the job you are applying for, and why an employer should consider you. Now is definitely not the time to be modest about your skills and accomplishments.

Examples:

1. "I have a reputation for being an excellent reporter who gets to the bottom of stories quickly."

2. "My excellent attitude and strong work ethic make me a valuable employee."

3. "With my performing arts background I am certain I would be a valuable addition to the Creative Arts Society."

Trying to write a short opening statement with this kind of impact may seem difficult at first. It is challenging, and requires practice, practice, practice. A great opening line will grab an employer's attention and create a great first impression. This is more than worth your time and effort.

 **Refer to the "Top 20 Openers . . . To Get Your Cover Letter Read" for more great openers!**

Work Space: Your Opening Sentence

n the Middle . . .

The Body

The body or content of the cover letter highlights skills you have to offer an employer. This is your opportunity to illustrate all the skills and personal attributes which make you ideal for the position, or worthy of an interview at the very least.

Remember: resist the temptation to say too much. Choose your words carefully. Brief is best!

When composing your letter, keep in mind that an employer may be faced with over one hundred letters to review. A brief, confident, and well-written letter is a blessing.

Should I Mention . . . ?

"The man who waits for just the right time to start never gets anywhere."

—Roger W. Babson

The body of your letter is basically composed of two elements:

→ What you can offer a potential employer

- your skills and personal attributes that would help you excel in the position.

→ Why you would like to work for the company

- how you would fit into the organization and why you would be successful and enjoy working there.

All this in one or two brief paragraphs! Challenging, yes . . . impossible, no!

Find a quiet location where you can work on developing your cover letter. Listening to the radio or watching television is too distracting and you will have trouble concentrating.

To be sure your cover letter is focused and relevant, try to determine what an employer values in an employee.

How?

- Speak directly with the employer.

  You may be surprised how much information an employer will give you regarding a specific position and its responsibilities.

- Interview employees with similar job duties.

  Check with people in your network who are similarly employed, or call a company which does similar work and speak with an employee. Ask what skills and personal characteristics people in this line of work possess.

 Be prepared before you make any phone calls. People are usually cooperative, but they are working and their time is limited.

- Thoroughly read the job advertisement.

  Employers must pay for the advertisements they place, so be assured the information they include is pertinent to the position.

  Sometimes an employer may ask for specifics, such as familiarity with a specific word-processing program or a diploma in visual arts.

  Be sure to signal that you have the specific skills in your cover letter. This is often the first thing an employer will look for. Not including it may mean your cover letter and resume don't make the initial cut.

 This does not mean you should avoid applying for a position if your qualifications are not an exact match. Employers advertise for the ideal candidate, but they often accept a range of applications around those standards. For example, your experience may make up for a lack of formal education or vice versa.

Work Space: Things to Mention

_____

_____

_____

_____

Dynamic Descriptions

Use words which add diversity and energy to your cover letters.

Examples:

ambitious

caring

committed

confident   . . . in my abilities

consistent(ly)   . . . provide quality service

cooperative

creative   . . . team member

determined

diligent(ly)   . . . work to produce results

diplomatic

dynamic   . . . public speaker

eager

effective

efficient(ly)   . . . implemented a new filing system

energetic   . . . sales person

enthusiastic

excellent

extensive   . . . experience working with

focused

innovative   . . . approach to

motivated

poised   . . . under pressure of deadlines

positive   . . . team member

productive

professional   . . . at all times when dealing with customers

proficient   . . . typist at 80 words per minute

quick

reliable
sensitive
sincere   . . . interest in
skilled/skillful
substantial
successful/success oriented
team player

Using dynamic words in your cover letter will catch an employer's attention.

Example:

"A motivated and conscientious nurse, I make patients' needs my priority. Patients have said I am quick, reliable, and caring, qualities I feel are essential to being an excellent nurse."

See the sample cover letters for further examples.

Work Space: Cover Letter Body

_____

_____

_____

_____

In the End . . .

The Closing:

This final section includes:

➡ A strong closing remark

➡ How an employer can reach you

➡ When you will follow up.

Stating you will follow up with an employer on a certain day after submitting your resume not only shows initiative and interest in the position, but gives you a legitimate reason to call for an update.

Example:

My education along with my experience would make me a productive addition to your team. I may be reached at 555-7489 and will call you November 10 to answer any questions you may have.

Avoid choosing Friday as the day for following up with employers. They are often winding down their workweek and may not be as open to your efforts as on another day.

Be absolutely certain to call back when you stated you would. Keep your call brief, positive, and professional—no matter who you speak with. A positive comment about your call is likely to be passed on, and a negative comment will definitely be passed on!

Work Space: Cover Letter Closing

_____

_____

_____

_____

Chapter 5

Employer Translations

Sometimes we get so involved writing a cover letter it becomes hard to imagine from an employer's viewpoint. It's a good idea to have someone else read your letter to provide another perspective and give feedback and suggestions.

"There can be no rainbow without a cloud and a storm."

—J.H.Vincent

Even if your letter is well-written and uses clear language and examples, there is still some room for misunderstandings and misinterpretation. There really is no way around this.

The following are phrases employers may interpret in a different way than you mean. Be aware of them when writing your own letters.

What You Say . . .		What the Employer Reads . . .
I am interested in any position at this time.	=	I am desperate for work and have no clear career goals.
To Whom It May Concern,	=	I don't have enough interest in the position to find out who is responsible for hiring.
Should you find me a suitable candidate for an interview . . .	=	I hope you find me qualified because I'm not sure if I am.
I am available for work immediately.	=	I am unemployed.

My qualifications exceed those required by this position.	=	I will gain nothing from this position and will move on as soon as something better comes along.
I hope you will take the time to read through my resume.	=	My resume is long and boring.
One should adopt work habits that are organized.	=	"I" haven't, but "one" should.
What you cannot see from my resume is that . . .	=	Because my resume is so out-dated all my experience is not on it.
I would be an asset to any position you have available.	=	I really have no idea what I want, or what your company has available.

 "Things do not change; we change."

—Henry David Thoreau

Chapter 6

Putting It All Together

By now you have the information you need, a strong opening sentence, the name of the person in charge of hiring, and descriptions of your own skills which will knock the socks off the employer. Now you must put it all into a letter which is not only organized and accurate, but visually appealing as well. Before you produce the final product, consider a few things.

 Make sure the layout of your cover letter is interesting. If it isn't, an employer may never get past it to see just how great your resume is.

Things to Consider

Once again, you must think of your cover letter as an extension of yourself! That's right—an extension of yourself. Since you cannot be there with the employer for the initial selection process, you must trust that your cover letter and resume will represent you accurately and professionally.

 'Three-tenths of a good appearance are due to nature; seven-tenths to dress.'

—Chinese proverb

There are a few additional details to consider. Just as you would consider your wardrobe and personal grooming before a personal interview, you should give close consideration to the following suggestions. Some of them may seem like ridiculous details, but taken together as part of the complete package they can add or detract from the presentation of your application. With the amount of competition out there, you want every advantage you can get.

Style

When developing a style for your cover letter you may consider:

Font

Be sure to choose a font, or type style, that is large, clear and easy to read.

Justification

Standard cover letters line up on the left, but if you would like to have a more formal, business-type cover letter consider using forced justification. This means your letter will line up on the left and right sides.

If you want to be creative, try centering your letter, but be sure it isn't too distracting. Remember, grabbing an employer's attention is good, but being too artistic can detract from your most important message: why you are right for the job.

Bolding/*Italics*

These are tools used to **focus** an employers attention on certain sections of your letter, an excellent idea. **Bolding** and *italics* can be used to highlight relevant **experience** that make you an ideal candidate for the position. *Do not use either of these too frequently in your letter or they will lose their effect.*

Overall appearance

Only you know whether using graphics or creating a personalized stationery for your cover letter is a good idea and one that will be well received by your profession. Your resume package faces a lot of competition before it is even read, so do not be afraid to be creative.

Paper

Color

Do not use fluorescent paper. While this paper may be catchy at first, it soon gets hard on the eyes—it's hard to read and generally irritating. Choose a softer color that will be easy on the eyes of an employer who has to look at one hundred resumes.

Your cover letter and resume are a package, so choose the same paper for both. If you don't have the same paper, choose a color and texture which compliment each other.

The more conservative the position for which you are applying, the more conservative the paper should be. This does not mean boring. Marbled paper with a hint of blue in it may be appropriate for a resume package designed for a creative consultant position, but not necessarily for a position as a lawyer.

There is a variety of professional looking paper available: cream, eggshell, gray, bluish and all sorts of paper with hints of color in them that are still subtle and professional.

Texture/Weight/Bond

The feel of the paper by any other name! Compare as many times as you like and you will find that a heavier, textured, quality stationery always makes your resume look better and more professional than standard weight, white paper. There is no denying that a quality resume and cover letter suggest a quality employee. That is the message you want to send to employers.

Make sure your printer has plenty of ink or a new ribbon. It won't make much difference what kind of paper you choose if the employer cannot read what is on it.

Do not fax your cover letter and resume to an employer. Most fax machines use the waxy light paper which rolls up as soon as it comes out of the machine. You don't want your resume on this.

Envelope size

If you are dropping your resume package off you should not even use an envelope. You should walk into the office with your resume in hand, intent on handing it, in person, to the individual responsible for hiring. However, if you must mail your resume package, choose an envelope large enough to accommodate your application without having to fold it.

Why?

Employers simply do not have the time, nor do they want the hassle of opening envelopes, unfolding resumes and trying to get the creases out of your resume to get it to lay flat in the pile with the rest. Anything that saves a busy employer time will be appreciated.

"You may not always be better than others but you can always be better than yourself."

—Ivan Panin

Paper Clips vs. Staples

Another important and, believe it or not, controversial detail! Our vote? Staples. The theory behind using paper clips was that it enabled the employer to unclip your resume and lay it all out to read it. Good idea, but the problem is that whether the employer wants the resume pages unclipped or not, they often end up that way.

Resumes end up in piles, and those piles get shuffled, stacked, knocked on the floor, filed, passed along, sorted, and resorted. Paper clips come off, staples don't. You certainly don't want half of your relevant work history on one person's desk and half on the floor in another office. If an employer wants to lay your resume all out on a desk they can do that with staples or clips.

Use staples.

Staple your resume and then place a paper clip on the first page. If an employer wants to take the staple out, you've already provided the clip!

Remember: above all else, your cover letter must look professional and be easy to read.

Checklist

Your cover letter is complete! But don't stop yet. There is one more step before printing the final draft.

Give your letter one last check to be sure everything is order. You'll be glad you did when you discover you forgot your phone number or notice the employer's name is spelled incorrectly.

The final check:

✓ Is your *name* on your letter and is it spelled correctly?

✓ Do you have your correct *phone number?* Be sure the employer doesn't have the wrong number when they call to ask you for an interview.

✓ Is the *employer's name* included with the correct spelling and the appropriate title, i.e. Ms., Mr., Miss? If the advertisement refers to the employer as M. Baker, don't assume it is Mr. or Ms. It's better to address a letter "Dear M. Baker" and not risk offending someone.

 It's a good idea to address a female employer as Ms., unless you know they prefer to be called Mrs. or Miss. Many women, married or not, prefer to be referred to in a way which makes no reference to their marital status.

✓ Have you included the *reference number* for the position you are applying for? If you are submitting an unsolicited resume, have you stated the type of work you are interested in?

✓ Make sure there are *no spelling errors.* If you are using a computer, use your spell checker. If not, use a dictionary. There is nothing more unprofessional than a cover letter with spelling errors.

✓ Check for *grammatical errors.* This can be tricky, so have a friend read your cover letter to check for "flow" problems and grammatical errors.

This is especially true if English is not your first language.

✓ Have you emphasized *key words*. If you want an employer's attention drawn to certain words or phrases in your letter, put them in bold or italicize them. Words which stand out are more likely to be remembered.

✓ Have you omitted *abbreviated words* and spelled them out completely? Write out "high density disk" rather than using HDD like you normally would. Now is not the time to prove your knowledge of abbreviations. Now is the time to show employers you know what they mean.

A strong closing remark leaves employers with a lasting impression of you. Try closing with a statement such as "I am confident my knowledge and experience would be an asset to your company," or "I look forward to working for a company which presents me with new challenges and further develops my skills."

✓ Include the *date*. Many employers keep old resumes on file and discard them after a certain period of time. By dating your cover letter you avoid your resume being discarded prematurely.

✓ Include the *date you will contact the employer*. Stating you will call the employer on a certain day not only shows initiative and interest in the position, it gives you a legitimate reason to call for an update on the competition.

Be sure to call back when you stated you would. If you don't, you not only seem uninterested, but also unlikely to follow through on things as an employee.

✓ Finally, be sure your cover letter is *interesting to look at and read*. Remember, you want to grab an employer's attention, so an eye-catching, concise letter is best. Do not bore employers with paragraph after paragraph of text.

After you print the final copy, remember to *sign* it. The personal touch at the end is a nice finish.

You have now completed your cover letter. Congratulations!

Chapter 7

The Good, The Bad, and The Ugly

Cover letters come in all forms. Like everything else, some are good and some are not so good. Let's look at cover letters that are good, bad, and ugly. Employers comments have been added to describe what they may be thinking when reading these letters.

"The world is full of cactus. But we don't have to sit on it."

—Will Foley

If you draw ideas from the good and drop ones you had that are bad or ugly, you will be well on your way to an effective cover letter.

The Good

Patricia Stapleton
123 Apple Way
Chelan, Washington
87667

Good, someone who tells me what they want!

I remember this person, she is really putting a lot of effort into trying to impress me. Good show!

Dear Mr. Baker,

Re: Automatic Dismantling Position

Thank you for taking the time to tell me about your company July 11. As we discussed, I have several years experience dismantling automobiles and am fast and efficient.

I respect the work your company does and look forward to the opportunity to join your team.

Sincerely,

Patricia Stapleton

Short, to the point, effective. What a refreshing cover letter.

(178) 555-0578

The Good

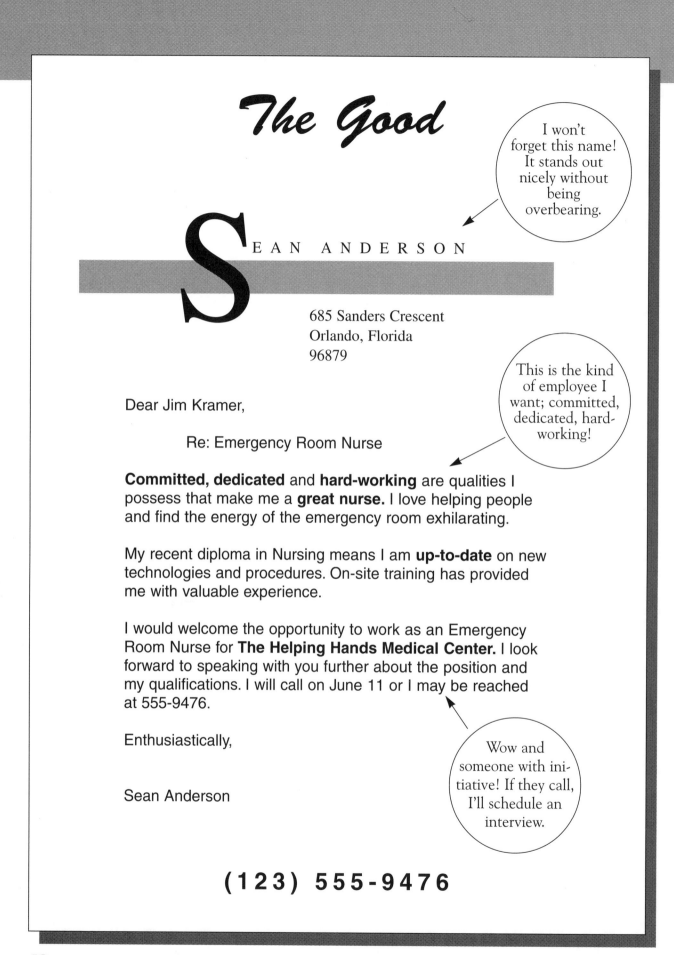

I won't forget this name! It stands out nicely without being overbearing.

SEAN ANDERSON

685 Sanders Crescent
Orlando, Florida
96879

Dear Jim Kramer,

Re: Emergency Room Nurse

This is the kind of employee I want; committed, dedicated, hard-working!

Committed, dedicated and **hard-working** are qualities I possess that make me a **great nurse.** I love helping people and find the energy of the emergency room exhilarating.

My recent diploma in Nursing means I am **up-to-date** on new technologies and procedures. On-site training has provided me with valuable experience.

I would welcome the opportunity to work as an Emergency Room Nurse for **The Helping Hands Medical Center.** I look forward to speaking with you further about the position and my qualifications. I will call on June 11 or I may be reached at 555-9476.

Enthusiastically,

Sean Anderson

Wow and someone with initiative! If they call, I'll schedule an interview.

(123) 555-9476

The Bad

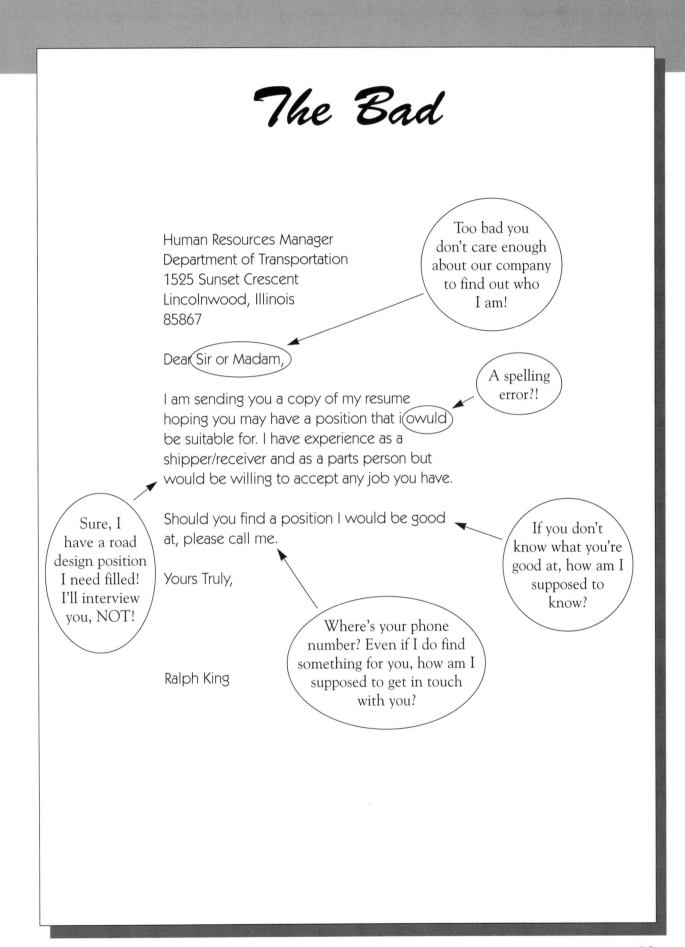

The Bad

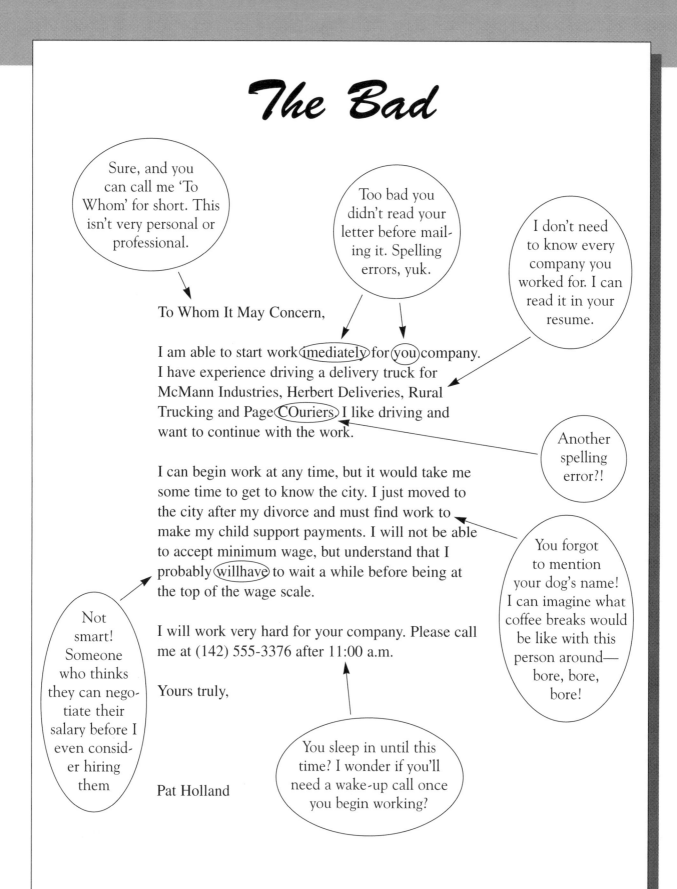

The Bad

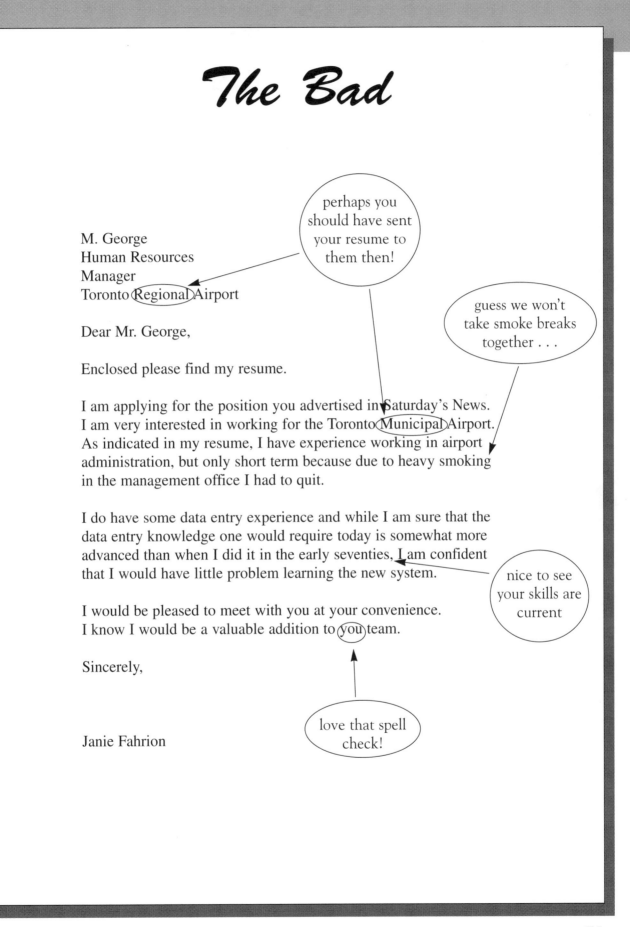

The Bad

any particular kind?

lots of basic knowledge here!

RE: EMPLOYMENT

TO WHOM IT MAY CONCERN:

so why should I read more?

I do not have any previous experience but I am a very quick learner. I have just completed a travel tourism course which taught me everything: destinations, reservations, ticketing, computers, geography, general office procedures, typing and tours. We were taught basic knowledge to work in a hotel such as reservations, room types, meal codes, booking terms, radio codes, international baggage, destination codes, currency codes, tour packages, accommodation types, hotel departments, and many other things. We were taught basic knowledge of computers in order to complete successful name fields, phone fields, ticketing fields, address fields and reference identifiers, availability and display codes, time, calculations and accessing information codes. The geography section included main attractions, codes and the basic knowledge of each country including map location. The tours section of our course taught me how to book tours with taxes, without taxes, deposits, total costs, commissionable totals, final payments, commission, net motorcoach and bus tours, popular abbreviations, cruise ship bookings and we practiced booking tours with many companies. Office procedures covered advertising, marketing principles, marketing planning, preparation for selling, sales styles, travel as a product, qualifying the client, closing the sale, telephone selling, typing, letter formats, banking procedures and filing.

way too much information!!

obviously not how to sell yourself!

   I am a hard working, dedicated, reliable, friendly, punctual person who would appreciate the chance to work with your company. I am available for an interview at your convenience.

Sincerely,

you forgot long-winded.

Garth Jamieson

till Bad

Yes, there are more, and they are still bad. Although these sentences seem absurd and ridiculous now, unless you read your cover letter out loud and really hear what you are telling an employer, you too could land somewhere in . . . 'the good, the bad, and the ugly!!'

 "The fool wonders, the wise man asks."

—Benjamin Disraeli

Cover 1

I am a little familiar with the operations of an insurance claim office as my mother has worked in the industry for many years. She currently is a customer service coordinator for Smith and Co. Insurance. She helps to set up new clients as well as train their staff. If I am hired for the position, my mother has already agreed to help me do some extra training at home so I can become familiar with your system more quickly.

"Maybe I should hire your Mother?"

Cover 2

With more than 20 years experience in general administration and financial assistance to senior management in quite a varied assortment of office environments, my duties and responsibilities have included: providing timely and knowledgeable information support; scheduling and transcribing senior management meeting minutes; creating, developing and implementing new and revised office procedures; creating standard letters and forms; liaison with government; training and supervision of administrative staff; assisting in complete budgeting and scheduling process, as required.

"Whew, all that in one breath!"

Cover 3

I have been employed with Airlines Are Us as a flight attendant since October of 1993. The majority of the local cabin crew and staff have just been served with notice of layoff due to a decrease in flights and I am currently seeking alternate employment. Employment in your office sounded interesting.

"Gee, I bet you'd stay around when the flights increased!"

Cover 4

I have a variety of experience and would enjoy working with your company in any capacity you see fit.

"So do you want to be a brain surgeon or a street cleaner?"

Cover 5

Handwritten on the bottom of the first page of a resume:
This is my application for the position you advertised Saturday, May 4, in The News.

"Couldn't find an extra piece of paper for the cover letter?"

Cover 6

I grew up on a farm east of town where my parents still live with my brother, grain farming and raising cattle.

"Exactly how does this relate to the office clerk position you are applying for?"

Cover 7

Call a mature, reliable, and hard-working individual today. Trust me, no employer has regretted making this call in the past. Do not become the first to regret not making the call. I can be reached anytime.

"Confidence is one thing, but good grief."

The Ugly

CLEVE RINGWOLD
CITY EMS
BOX 465
LINCOLNWOOD

RE: EMERGENCY MEDICAL TECHNICIAN

I HAVE RECENTLY COMPLETED THE EMT-A PROGRAM AND
HAVE A GREAT INTEREST IN WORKING WITH YOUR POSITIVE
AND SUCCESSFUL TEAM.

MY EDUCATION, RIDE ALONGS AND VOLUNTEER EXPERIENCES
HAVE PREPARED ME EFFECTIVELY FOR EMPLOYMENT IN THE
FIELD AND WITHIN A SHORT TIME I AM CONFIDENT I WOULD
BECOME A VALUABLE ASSET TO YOUR TEAM. MY LEADERSHIP
SKILLS AND WILLINGNESS TO TAKE ON RESPONSIBILITY AND
CHALLENGES IS STRONG. ONE OF MY GREATEST ASSETS,
HOWEVER, IS MY ABILITY TO INTERACT WITH EMPLOYEES
AND PATIENTS, INSTILLING IN THEM CONFIDENCE AND TRUST.

I HAVE A STRONG DESIRE TO CONTINUE MY EDUCATION AND
INCREASE MY LEVEL OF SKILL THROUGH ADDITIONAL TRAIN-
ING, DAY TO DAY EXPERIENCES AND WORKING WITH A PROFES-
SIONAL TEAM. I LOOK FORWARD TO FURTHER DISCUSSING THIS
OPPORTUNITY AND HOW I CAN APPLY MY SKILLS TO IT. I MAY
BE REACHED AT 555-9876 FOR A PERSONAL INTERVIEW AT YOUR
CONVENIENCE.

SINCERELY,

GERARD GAGNON

lots to offer, too bad it hurts my eyes to read about it!

Ya!! and this is easy to read . . .

The Ugly

Great, I'm now a blank to be filled in!

Dear   Mr. James Tofield

    Re: Postal Carrier Position

Do you plan to carry mail with a partner?

I am a hard worker who strives to do a good job. I have good people skills and work well as a team member.

I have a diploma in Business Administration and 6 years experience in the work force.

I look forward to the opportunity to work for Round County Postal Services   and may be reached at 555-8968.

The typing looks different! He didn't even take the time to use the same typewriter when filling in the blanks.

Sincerely,

Raymondo Plantsky

The Ugly

like I have the time and energy to read all of this?

To Whom it May Concern:

I would like to submit my resume for your perusal with respect to the position for Junior Accountant with your professional and successful firm.

spaces?? anywhere

I am currently enrolled in the Certified General Accounting program at the City College and hope to complete the requirements for certification. I would be pleased to present you with another copy of my resume and my transcripts at that time. I have learned a lot at school and I have a lot of experience from prior to returning to school and I am certain you would find me proficient in the following:

does this say anything in particular?

General Office Procedures:
I have considerable office experience as I worked as an executive assistant prior to going back to school. My skills include: typing, filing, operating a multi-line phone system efficiently, scheduling management meetings, taking minutes, reorganizing filing systems, data entry and basic computer skills.

Bookkeeping skills:
In some of the jobs I had as an office worker I was responsible for maintaining the books in an efficient and organized manner. (So I thought I would take the plunge, go back to school and make it official!) I am knowledgeable in general ledgers, business taxation, invoicing, accounts payables and accounts receivables, some computer accounting packages, and inventory control. Additionally you will find me skilled in the use of various office machines: photocopier, fax machine, typewriter, adding machine, calculator and basic computers. Thank you for your consideration in this matter.

I hate hyphens

how nice!

Sincerely,

Desmond Jones

The Ugly

Dear Ms. Cramer

I am applying for the Child Care Worker position at Wee Care Day Care. I am a trained and experienced child care worker who loves children.

Planning creative programs which stimulate children and designing crafts to encourage imagination are two of my strong skills. I would bring enthusiasm and a love for my work to your center.

I may be reached at 555-9846.

Yours truly,

Alexis Stanton

She crammed everything into the top corner of the page, why not use the whole page?

Was the type supposed to be cute? It looks childish and unprofessional.

The content of the letter is good, but it sure looks ugly.

Chapter 8

Sample Cover Letters

Review the content and style of the cover letters on the following pages and see what you can use in your own cover letters. Practice your letter writing skills and be creative. Your letters will never come across as boring or routine again!

"He who is outside his door already has a hard part of his journey behind him."

—Dutch proverb

Monique Manon
#254, 67 Street West
Quebec City, PQ
555-4367

<u>Re: Sales Professional</u>

Areas of Expertise:

- skilled cold caller
- professional telephone manner
- dynamic presenter
- energetic and persistent

I am certain you would find me to be a valuable asset to your team. I will call April 4 to discuss the position with you further.

Sincerely,

Monique Manon
555-4367

 More frequently companies are asking for applicants to fax resumes. Do not use the comment section of the fax cover sheet or a handwritten note on the bottom of your resume in lieu of a cover letter!

Chloe Brandler
Community Pool
Cherry Point, NC

Dear Ms. Brandler,

I have been progressively involved in aquatics for the past five years and wish to be considered for the position of Lifeguard/Instructor with the Community Pool.

My technical skills are exceptional and I have demonstrated the ability to provide both high quality swim instruction and pool supervision. I relate well to pre-schoolers, children, and adults, individually and in groups.

Thank you for your consideration and I look forward to a personal interview at your convenience. I may be reached at **555-3827.**

Sincerely,

Trent Bergess

S AMUEL JACKSON

15468 85A Street
San Antonio, Texas
96707
(123) 555-4739

Jordan Debaji
Human Resources Manager
Debaji & Whitford Engineering Inc.
476 Ritt Avenue
San Antonio, Texas
89768

Dear Mr. Debaji,

Re: Junior Engineer Position

As you suggested during our telephone conversation on May 28, I am submitting my resume for the position of Junior Engineer.

With three years experience as a civil engineer, I have developed a solid understanding of the business yet am eager to continue growing and expanding my knowledge of the industry. I have worked on a variety of projects and received compliments on my work habits and ethics, as well as my ability to interact with clients.

I feel that not only would your company provide me with new and exciting challenges, but my experience, energy, and skills will be of benefit to you.

I may be reached at (123) 555-4739 and will contact you on June 11 to answer any questions you may have.

I look forward to hearing from you.

Samuel Jackson

Grant Peterson
54 Gagliardi Way
Burnaby, BC
B4R 6Y7
555-9876

Ms. Keets-Anderson,

My active involvement developing and implementing individual education plans on an interdisciplinary team makes me an excellent candidate for the contract position available with your school.

In addition to working with children with a variety of special needs, I have also extended my efforts to include educating parents through home visits on language stimulation techniques. I am currently expanding my sign-language vocabulary, thus increasing my effectiveness in the classroom.

Thank you for considering my application for what I know will be an exciting and rewarding position. I will contact you the week of January 10, or I may be reached at 555-9876.

Sincerely,

Grant Peterson

Jack Schnieder
184 West Lane
Key Largo, Florida
85876

Dear Ahmid Somji,

Re: **Social Worker Position**

Professional and **caring** are two words I use to describe myself and these are reflected in my studies, occupational choices, and employment history.

I have **extensive experience** working with troubled youth and find the work **challenging** and **fulfilling**.

My **Social Work Degree** and numerous Youth Development Workshops make me **well qualified.**

I look forward to further discussing the Social Work Position and will call you on November 16 to answer any questions you may have. I may also be reached at **(121) 555-9958.**

Enthusiastically,

Jack Schnieder

(121) 555-9568

Tonia Berck
Program
Co-ordinator
Battleford House
6470 Victrolla Drive
Battleford, SK

Re: Coordinator, Wellness and Independence Program

Dear Tonia Berck,

I have recently published a series of papers, The Contagious Positive Attitude, for an American publisher and have considerable in-class experience as a wellness consultant and career counsellor. I am a dynamic and adaptable facilitator with experience coordinating and developing a pilot project for a federally funded Independent Living program.

I currently volunteer with the Rape Relief and Women's Shelter and have a great desire to use my experience to further participate in the pro-active stand necessary to resolve some of the issues facing women today.

I will call the week of January 30 to answer any questions you may have regarding my qualifications or I may be reached at 555-9087 at your convenience. I look forward to meeting you in person.

Sincerely,

Bailey Freeman

Bailey Freeman
14 Helmsley
Battleford, SK
555-9087

DANA BROADMOOR

re: Training Assistant, City Police Service

Dear Mr. P. Bosworth,

I am enclosing my resume outlining my skills in: instruction, training, writing and computer applications. I am certain my combination of skills and personal experience will make me a valuable addition to your team.

Adult Instruction: computer applications and communication workshops
- *Instructed MicroSoft Word, Excel 4.0, SuperPaint and MacDraw in a lab environment*
- *Prepared and facilitated workshops on Teamwork and Planning*

Alcohol and Drug Awareness sessions for Young Offenders
- *Group leader for awareness sessions*
- *Volunteer Probation Officer*

Design and Creation of Newsletters and Brochures
- *Designed and created trade show displays*
- *Produced papers in relation to Criminal Justice system for use in Canadian Universities*

I will bring experience and a sound work ethic to your organization and know I would contribute much to this position. I look forward to meeting you in person and may be reached at **555-0460.**

Sincerely,

Dana Broadmoor

555-0460

December 11

Human Resources
City of Wichita Police Department
768 Avid Landing
Wichita, Kansas

Dear Mr. Wesley,

I am a highly motivated, athletic, and energetic person who strives
for excellence in everything I do. My drive and ambition would be
an asset to the City of Wichita Police Department.

My police training is extensive and ongoing. I have a diploma in law
enforcement and have taken numerous self-defense, communication,
and negotiating courses. I am a black belt in Karate and feel my
skills and discipline would be an asset to your police department.

Becoming a law enforcement officer is my goal and I know I would
do an excellent job.

I look forward to hearing from you and may be reached at (154)
555-9765. I will contact you the week of December 18 to respond
to any questions you may have.

Enthusiastically,

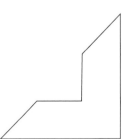

Jane Randall

J a m e s   L a u

Re: ELECTRONICS TECHNOLOGIST

Dear Ms. Fraser,

My considerable experience includes: **assembling, testing,** and **troubleshooting** of electronic circuit boards. Additionally, I am familiar with computer application software such as **AutoCad**, Windows, and Excel.

With my qualifications, interpersonal skills, and sincere interest in the industry, I am certain you would quickly find me a valuable asset to your organization.

I would appreciate the opportunity to meet with you at your earliest convenience and may be reached at **555-3627**.

Sincerely,

James Lau

 To draw added attention to certain qualifications, put in bold or italicize specific words. Be careful not to do this too much or you will lose the effect.

James Lau, 890 Schoolhouse Avenue, Flagstaff, AZ, 90543, **555-3627**

Raoul Jafar
87 Cummings Way
Grand Island, Nebraska
90098

Dear Charlene Davis,

   Re: Junior Broadcasting Position

Exceptional *communication skills* and *witty conversation*
make me a great choice for the 'Late Hour' Radio
broadcasting position.

"Raoul is humorous and engaging to listen to and keeps
everyone sitting on the edge of their seats." "Although Raoul's
job description did not include formal presentations, his
entertaining manner and ability to draw people's attention
encouraged us to place him in charge of company
promotions." This is how previous employers describe
my communication skills.

I look forward to meeting with you and auditioning with
497 KV Radio. I will contact you on September 4 to answer
any questions or may be reached at (176) 555-5345.

Raoul Jafar

555-8976

andrea willingdon

April 18, 1995
Rodney Fung
Travel Innovations
P.O. Box 4673
Baton Rouge

Re: Travel Consultant

Dear Mr. Fung,

I am presently seeking employment in or around the Baton Rouge area. My office skills are superior and I am familiar with the workings of an efficient business office. I have a willingness to learn, enjoy a challenge in my career, and am always working to enhance my skills.

My father, stepmother and brother all work for major airlines, so I have been fortunate enough to travel extensively and explore the workings of the travel industry.

I am excited by the prospect of a career change and the opportunity of growing with your company and look forward to discussing your company's needs. I may be reached at your convenience at 555-8530.

Sincerely,

Andrea Willingdon

5 5 5 - 8 5 3 0

Richard Pollings
8b, Rue Maison
Winnipeg, Manitoba
555-0926

Ms. R. Sutton
Human Resources
Regional Airfield
Organization
Winnipeg, Manitoba

Dear Ms. Sutton,

This letter is to express my sincere interest in opportunities with the Regional Airfield Organization.

Previously I was employed as a flight coordinator with a commuter airline based in Toronto, Ontario. Additionally, my experience includes working as an accountant, accounting assistant and an inquiry clerk with a major Healthcare company in Manitoba. With more than four years experience with a commuter airline and the successful completion of the air Carrier/Airport Management Program combined with a Business Administration degree, I have a lot to offer.

Thank you for your attention. I would be happy to provide any further information you may require and look forward to meeting you in person. I may be reached at 555-0926.

Sincerely,

Richard Pollings

Lots of white space on the page makes a letter much easier to read and more pleasing to look at.

Richard Shank   March 15
Staffing Advisor
Human Resources Division
Muttart Surround

Allan Lang
Windy Avenue
Hood River, Oregon
74435
(190) 555-8844

Dear Mr. Shank,

    Re: Plant Operator Position
    (as outlined in Opportunities #98)

Experience, knowledge and **dedication** make me an excellent
candidate for the *Plant Operator* position at Muttart Surround.

I would give my best as an operator and would be proud to be a
part of the Muttart team.

I will keep in touch and you may contact me at **(190) 555-8844.**

Sincerely,

Allan Lang

Ms. Laine,

I am seeking part-time employment in the customer service industry and am very interested in the position your company has to offer.

My background includes 11 years experience serving customers in a variety of positions. I sincerely enjoy meeting new people and performing a variety of tasks offering both challenge and satisfaction.

I have enclosed my resume for your review and will contact you to answer any questions you may have.

Sincerely,

Mai-Ling Low

555-0987
Mai-Ling Low

Yvonne Cardinal
18873 112 Avenue
Omaha, Nebraska
66587

Dear Mohammed Ahmin,

Re: Sales Clerk Position

Helping customers **coordinate** their wardrobe and **building repeat clientele** would be my goals if given the opportunity to work as a Sales Clerk for Lookin' Good Fashions.

I have **excellent public relation skills** and have worked with cash registers in the past.

The possibility of joining your sales team interests me and I would appreciate hearing from you should a position become available. I will keep in touch and may be reached at (109) 555-0076.

Sincerely,

Yvonne Cardinal

(109) 555-0076

Ron Milne
Operations Manager
Food Chain Restaurants of Canada
Saskatoon, SK

Re: **Community Relations Representative**

Mr. Milne,

Having built a solid network in private, not-for-profit, and government organizations in my current position, I am confident I could use and expand that network as your Community Relations Representative for Food Chain Restaurants.

I am familiar with Saskatoon and surrounding area and have a broad knowledge of varied companies and industries and their role in the city. **Innovation** and **creativity** are personal strengths and I have been responsible for both advertising and marketing in several past positions.

Food Chain is a progressive company committed to the community it serves and I would welcome the challenge of using my **communication skills** to represent and promote your company. I look forward to meeting you in person, Mr. Milne, and may be reached at 555-9220.

Sincerely,

Bobbi Mueller

Robert Quincy
Box 1678
Winnipeg, Manitoba
Y7U 9KO
(176) 555-1164

January 13

Dear Valerie Barnell,

Re: Laborer Position

I have a **reputation** for being a **reliable** and **enthusiastic** employee. I am **hard-working** and an **eager team member.**

I look forward to joining your company with the **confidence** that my **skills** and **knowledge** gained over the past 19 years will be of benefit to your company.

I look forward to **committing** myself to a reputable firm like SeRupt Industries.

Sincerely,

Robert Quincy

(176) 555-1164

Festival Promotions
82 Palm Crescent
Venice Beach, CA

Dear Blaine Devon,

With my strong oral and written communication skills and
dynamic **public relations** abilities, I am certain I would be
a valuable addition to the Festival Promotions Team.

I have considerable **media** experience working in both
television and radio, behind the scenes and on air. Having
developed numerous advertising packages from trade
show displays to program information letters and company
service portfolios, I excel in any creative environment.

I sincerely enjoy working with a creative, professional
team under the constant challenge of meeting **deadlines**. I
would welcome the opportunity to work for the largest of
Venice Beach's summer festivals and look forward to
discussing the position further.

Sincerely,

Derek Stubbings
555-0976

Pat Walters
Shapiro Designs
76 West Meuse
Englewood, Colorado
87515

Dear Pat Walters,

RE: Interior Designer Position

Determined, hard-working, a quick study; these are qualities I possess
which would make me an excellent interior designer.

I have any eye for fashion and a flair for coordinating colors, material,
and furniture. Many friends and associates have called on my skills to
help design rooms in their homes. Along with my resume, I have attached
pictures of several rooms I coordinated.

If you want an employee with energy, creativity, and a strong desire to
please, I am the one for you. I will contact you in one week to answer
questions you may have and look forward to the opportunity to meet with
you in person. I may be reached at (195) 555-2596.

Thank you for your consideration,

Pamela Tate

Sydney Banks

#312, 1078
Hardwood Avenue
Indianapolis, IN
555-8097

Dear Marvin Freidman,

I am very interested in the employment opportunity your firm is offering. I have a strong desire to enter the field of graphic design and would be pleased to be considered for this position.

My formal training is in photography and I am interested in developing myself in other creative industries. I enjoy working with design and have a keen eye for color with many new ideas.

My communication skills are excellent and I would sincerely enjoy the challenge of assisting clients in making choices that would best represent their company. My photography experience would be an asset, as principals of design are similar in both photography and graphic art.

I am a quick learner and would work hard to excel in this position. I look forward to further discussing your needs and may be reached at 555-8097.

Sincerely,

Sydney Banks

Ricardo Piccolo
Owner
T T Driver's Training
Salt Lake City, Utah

Attention Ricardo Piccolo,

Re: Manager Position

I am a dedicated employee who takes pride in a job well done. I have extensive Managerial experience and would transfer these skills to T T Driver's Training.

Along with managing my own business I have several years experience driving and know the importance of safe and attentive driving.

I would look forward to joining your organization and will contact you the week of August 29. I may be reached at (198) 555-0879.

Yours truly,

Terri Robinson

Arthur Malloy
Director
ABC Corporation
Big Town, Stateside
93846

Jane Royston
2378 89 Street
Big Town, Stateside
97563

Dear Arthur Malloy,

I am very interested in the position of Customer Service Representative
with ABC Corporation and feel my strong organizational and
communication skills would be a definite asset to your team.

As indicated in my resume, I have many transferable skills and valuable
experiences gained from my years in retail sales. I am confident in
my ability to work with people and add creative ideas and techniques
to your sales team.

I would appreciate the chance to meet with you in person to discuss your
personnel needs now or in the future. I may be reached at 555-3833. I
will call the week of September 3 to answer any questions you may have
regarding my qualifications.

Sincerely,

Jane Royston

Marion Glier
Life Choice
4th Avenue NW
Des Moines, Iowa

Brian Youngman
816, 8 Street West
Des Moines, Iowa
555-1234

Dear Marion Glier,

My ongoing interest in serving the developmentally delayed and/or handicapped individuals leads me to apply for a position with your organization.

My skills and experience as a rehabilitation practitioner are especially suited to work with persons requiring close personal attention.

I would appreciate the opportunity to speak with you regarding how I can be of service to your organization. I may be reached at 555-1234 or a message may be left at the same number. I look forward to meeting you in person and will call the week of November 25 to answer any questions you may have regarding my qualifications.

Sincerely,

Brian Youngman

Harriet Nordstrom
Manager, Human Resources
JBS Accounting
Trenton Avenue
Toronto, ON

_____

Amanda Grimsley
8347 Stewart Crescent
Toronto, ON

_____

Dear Harriet Nordstrom,

My extensive experience in computerized accounting makes me a
valuable candidate for the accounting position. As an employee in the
accounting field, Accounts Payable, Accounts Receivable, General
Ledger, Trial Balance and Month End Statements were among my key
responsibilities.

I am presently enrolled in a CMA Program and have successfully
completed three computerized accounting courses. I am certain I can
successfully apply my computer knowledge to your company's computer
system.

I have well-developed organizational and communication skills and am a
dependable employee, consistently achieving well above expectations. I
am willing to go beyond my duties to take on other responsibilities.

Sincerely,

Amanda Grimsley

Mandi Potamick
67 Rainforest Crescent
Miami, FL
98076

Dear Dr. Blair,

Through my practicum experiences, I have found working with severely delayed and disordered children to be both challenging and rewarding work. Your innovative collaboration between Speech Language Pathologists and Teachers provides an ideal learning environment for language disordered students. My clinical experience and excellent interpersonal skills would definitely be well suited to working in this dynamic school setting.

Thank you for considering my application. I will contact you the week of March 9 to answer any questions you may have regarding my suitability for this position.

Sincerely,

Mandi Potamick

 Make a point of reading your letter out loud before making a final copy. You will be surprised at the different perspective it will give you.

P.J. Atwell
Senior Fitness Consultant
Muscles Training Center
Grand Rapids, Michigan

Dear P.J. Atwell,

As a recent high school graduate, I would bring enthusiasm, energy and eagerness to your company.

I have been involved in fitness for a number of years and my goal is to become a fitness consultant. I am interested in a position where I can use my athletic knowledge to help others with their workouts.

I may be reached at 555-9878 and look forward to hearing from you.

Eagerly,

Careen Rinka

Dear Mr. Matias,

I possess many skills that would greatly benefit your organization:

- *formal sales training*
- *excellent customer service skills*
- *diverse computer training and experience*
- *typing speed of 80 wpm*

My professional attitude and enthusiasm would make me a valuable addition to your team. I look forward to meeting you in person and may be reached at 555-3734.

Sincerely,

Janie Nordic
555-3734

"Don't ever slam a door. You might want to go back."

—Don Herold

Bruce Caporale
Owner
Cafe Majestic
Madison, Wisconsin

Dear Bruce Caporale,

Re: Waiter Position

My excellent *people skills* and *strong work ethic* make me a valuable employee.

I am available for part-time or permanent work and look forward to the opportunity to become a waiter in your cafe. I may be reached at 555-4359.

Eagerly awaiting your call.

Bhajan Deol

 You only have one chance to make a first impression. Take the time to make a great one!

Company xyz
Suite 675, 10035 - 108 Avenue
Edmonton, AB
Y7U 8G6

Dear Georgia Simms,

<u>*Re: Executive Assistant*</u>

I am an individual with outstanding office administrative abilities. As a *conscientious* and responsible employee, my knowledge and experience in office administration contribute to my capability of working with minimal supervision.

I assert strong *organizational skills* in arranging and *prioritizing* my workload to effectively perform my duties in a timely manner.

My *computer skills* include proficient use of WordPerfect 5.1, Lotus, and Excel. Additionally I have a working knowledge of accounting principles and the accompanying computer programs.

I may be reached at 555-9227 and look forward to discussing my suitability for this position.

Sincerely,

Anita Chow

Do not count on spell check alone to catch errors in your letter. 'He' is a word to the spell checker but "applying for 'he' position of . . ." doesn't make a lot of sense.

Kelly Lawrence
45 Mason Street
Williston, Vermont
56564
(177) 555-6943

July 13

Dear Frank Lackey,

Re: Bank Teller Position

Accurate, dependable, and trustworthy are personal qualities
which would make me a good bank teller.

I have worked with the public as a retail clerk and enjoy the
contact with people. My cash skills are excellent and I
consistently closed out my till balanced.

I may be reached at 555-4323 and will contact you the week
of July 20 to answer any questions you may have.

Looking forward to hearing from you,

Kelly Lawrence

(177) 555-6943

Conclusion

You are now an expert at writing cover letters! No more boring letters which say where you saw a position advertised and offer little information about your skills and talents. You now descriptively and concisely outline what you have to offer, and in a way that is pleasing to look at and is effective. Congratulations!

If you have your resume ready, you can now begin submitting application packages with the confidence that what you say is important to employers. Work as hard at your job search as you have developing your cover letters and you are sure to locate a job—soon!